# HEALTHY GROWTH
## FOR THE
## FAMILY BUSINESS

JENNIFER M. PENDERGAST, PH.D

Family Enterprise Publishers
P.O. Box 4356
Marietta, GA 30061-4356
800-551-0633
www.efamilybusiness.com

ISBN: 1-891652-17-6
© 2006

## Other Titles in the Family Business In-Depth Series

---

## Healthy Growth For The Family Business
## By Jennifer M. Pendergast, Ph.D

Copyright 2006 by Family Enterprise Publishers
       1220-B Kennestone Circle
       Marietta, GA 30066
       www.efamilybusiness.com

# Contents

# Exhibits

# I. Introduction: Pathways to Intelligent Growth

Family-owned Wawa Inc. is one of the largest convenience-store chains in the country and continues on a path of aggressive growth, with sales exceeding $1 billion. Based in Wawa, Pennsylvania, the company owns and operates more than 540 stores in five states and plans to open nearly 200 more stores within the next five years. Founded by Grahame Wood in 1964, the chain emerged out of waning Wood family textile and dairy-farming businesses that dated back to the early 19th century.[1]

In 2004, brothers Joe and Ray Fletcher retired, ending the long run of family involvement in a small but popular enterprise on the Potomac River known as Fletcher's Boat House. Under a contract with the National Park Service, the Washington, D.C., concession rented boats and bikes and sold bait and tackle. Although it stayed small, for nearly 150 years it supported four generations of Fletchers, who counted several U.S. presidents among their customers. While members of the fifth generation opted not to continue the family enterprise, its on-going success shows that small businesses, even without growth, can provide nice streams of profit across generations.[2]

Family businesses find many different paths to success. Some, like Wal-Mart become among the world's largest businesses. Others, like Fletcher's Boat House happily serve a limited market.

Whether a business remains small or grows large, **every family business at some time or other is faced with issues that center around growth**. If you are a member of a business-owning family, you may ask such questions as: Do we want this business to grow? Why should we grow it? Is it capable of growing? What sacrifices will growth require? What sacrifices will we make if we don't grow?

How these questions are answered in a family business are different than how they are answered in other companies. Decision-makers in publicly traded companies are typically focused on building their own wealth and the wealth of the shareholders. Leaders of family firms take into consideration not just the business but also that the business'growth will affect the business and the family. Family business leaders want to provide income and wealth, but are equally concerned about how growth will affect family members, employees, members of the community and other stakeholders in terms of their careers, their relationships and their well being.

Growth in a family business is a complicated matter. Growth issues may become most critical in times of transition, when a business is grappling with succession from one generation to the next, when family desires for cash compete with investing in company growth or when trends in the competitive environment necessitate change.

1

*Healthy Growth for the Family Business* is aimed at helping members of family businesses sort out the issues associated with growth and arrive at decisions that are best for the business and the family. This book defines "healthy growth" as growth that is sustainable and profitable.

> ..."*healthy growth*" *as growth that is sustainable and profitable.*

While you read the following pages, you will expand the way you think about growth. You will see that growth can mean different things to different people, and not just in terms of increases in sales and profits. The ways some family business owners look at growth will offer inspiration and spur creativity as you seek answers for your own company.

Others in your business and the family will benefit from reading this book and we encourage you to share it with them. They include members of your senior management team, shareholders, your board of directors, family members not involved in day-to-day operations, and younger family members who may one day be involved as employees or owners. When these people have a better understanding of the issues involved in growth, they can support you in moving the family business in the direction it needs to go.

This book will provide you with practical knowledge. It will help you decide whether to grow and, if so, what type and amount of growth you want. It will enable you to be realistic about your company's potential for growth and about the consequences of the failing to grow. You will learn to avoid the dangers of overestimating your company's ability to grow or underanticipating the company's need for growth. This book will also help you determine how best to reach your growth goals. In addition, it will serve as a useful tool in facilitating the important conversations that you must have with others about issues surrounding growth.

It is not the intent of this book to persuade you that growth is appropriate or the only objective for your business. That's for you and your family to decide. What this book *will* do is give you some pragmatic guidelines for thinking about the issues and for steps you can take if you decide growth is right for your business. Hopefully, what is offered here will help family businesses thrive and be healthy.

# II. Should We Grow or Stay the Same?

Growth is viewed as an imperative by most businesses.

"Grow or die!" is the battle cry of many authorities on business. "You're either going to grow your business or you're going to go backwards," says DeNean Stafford III, the second-generation CEO of Stafford Development Company, a holding company in Tifton, Georgia. Having been presented with the opportunity to run his family's company, Stafford insists that "just to manage the status quo would be heresy." Besides, he adds, "it wouldn't be much fun, either."

*Growth is the oxygen of business, the key to business life or death.*

In his book, *Double-Digit Growth: How Great Companies Achieve It—No Matter What*, Michael Treacy maintains, "Growth is the oxygen of business, the key to business life or death. Growing enterprises thrive; shrinking companies vanish."[3]

In many cases a business must grow to survive. But, many family businesses such as Fletcher's Boat House, prefer to remain small and do so successfully. One of my colleagues recently identified over 3000 family businesses in the United States that have survived for over a century. Those businesses averaged 30 employees. They have survived while remaining small. You have a choice, and this chapter will help you explore what's right for you.

A heavy an emphasis on the "grow or die" attitude can put pressure on a family business to focus on growth at all costs and not necessarily for sound reasons. Many businesses have grown themselves into risky situations which can result in lower profits, reduced distributions or having to sell off part of the business to survive.

"I was taught never to grow for growth's sake. Volume does not equal profit," says Jon Deeny, the third-generation leader of Deeny Construction Company in Seattle. "Some of the biggest construction companies have drowned in red ink."[4]

Growth that's too rapid can get out of control, putting undue strain on the business, management and employees. But lacking any sense of pressure to grow can also be equally unhealthy. When owners feel no urgency to grow, they may not be taking the necessary steps to improve the business. Owners may become complacent about growth because they have been successful in the past. If a family business has enjoyed protection from competition, the owner may not be aware of changes in the marketplace and may wake up one day to find that the business is too far behind the competition to catch up. Consider, the family hardware stores wiped out by Home Depot and Lowe's because they weren't able to find a way to successfully differentiate themselves.

What is needed instead of either extreme—an attitude of growth at any cost or a complacency about growth—is a balance between these points of view. This means taking into consideration how much growth (if any) is right for your business and how you're going to achieve it.

The starting point is to think through the reasons for either growing or maintaining your business without growth.

*...taking into consideration how much growth is right for your business and how you're going to achieve it.*

## Considerations Unique to Family Firms

There are solid reasons for business growth that are applicable to both family and non-family firms. Both find that growth generates career opportunities that helps attract and retain talented employees. In many industries, businesses understand that their competitors are focused on growth and unless they are too, the competition may steal their customers through superior service, better product offerings or more aggressive sales tactics. Furthermore, customers continue to make new demands and businesses must grow to meet them. Growth also provides economies of scale allowing businesses to be more competitive.

There are a number of reasons for growth that are unique to family firms:

1. Growth creates jobs for qualified family members and helps them to fulfill their aspirations.

2. Profitable growth offers the business the ability to support the family financially as it expands, increasing the family's financial worth and providing financial opportunities to family members who may not want to remain as owners.

3. Growth can help assure sufficient funds to allow family members to cash out. As a business transitions through generations, not all owners will want to remain as owners. Inheritors of stock may wish to sell their shares so they can pursue other goals.

4. Growth expands the owning family's exit options. If a family decides it wants to sell the business or spin off part of it, the company needs to be of a sufficient size to attract outside investors or buyers.

5. Growth enhances a family company's ability to attract excellent non-family employees.

Managers of non-family firms may have good reason to envy their peers in family firms. These managers may feel pressure to grow the business in ways that are outside of their control. Investors in either private or public non-family companies push for growth to meet their investment expectations, often regardless of the businesses' ability to grow or the potential damage that rapid growth can cause.

Owners and managers of family businesses, on the other hand, have more control over their own destiny. Owners and family members in the business usually have a long-term perspective and are concerned about the damage from too rapid growth. They exercise more patience when it comes to getting a return on their investment.

**EXHIBIT 1** ▌▌▌▌▌▌▌▌▌▌▌▌▌▌▌▌▌▌▌▌▌▌▌▌▌▌

## *10 Reasons for Expanding Your Family Firm*

1. To create jobs for family members and help them to fulfill their aspirations.

2. To support the family as its size increases.

3. To increase the financial worth of the family.

4. To enable the business to provide liquidity to owners.

5. To help the business fund retirement for family employees and owners.

6. To expand the family's exit options by making the business attractive to investors and buyers.

7. To enhance the company's ability to attract and retain well-qualified non-family employees.

8. To fend off the competition.

9. To enable the business to meet expanding customer needs.

10. To do business more efficiently by providing economies of scale.

## Deciding Not To Grow

Despite the attraction of expansion, many family business owners choose not to grow. They tend to be more "risk averse" as most of their families' wealth is tied up in the business.

Another common reason for not growing is because the company's leader wants to retain operational control. Growth may require bringing in people from outside the family to help run the business. That could mean sharing private information and letting others make decisions. Such things may require more trust than some family business owners can muster.

Family business owners' desire for control may also extend to financial and ownership matters. It's often not possible to grow a business without bringing in money from outside in the form of investors or debt. Not all owners want to take that step. In such cases, the business's growth is limited by how much cash the business can generate internally. If substantial growth requires building a new plant and the business owner is unwilling to borrow the money to build it, the plant will not be built and the expansion will not be realized.

Still another major deterrent to growth can be that the owning family just doesn't know *how* to grow the business. If a family member working in the family firm has never worked anywhere else, they may not have gained the skills needed to oversee a larger enterprise. "How could I manage that many employees?" they ask. "How could we possibly support that many customers?" Perhaps they haven't automated or invested in new technology to the extent required to grow a business because they haven't experienced or seen it done previously. Having the opinion, "doing things the way we've always done it," will eventually limit growth.

Growth can also be slow or nonexistent in some companies because the family has emotional ties to a particular segment of the business and are unable to let it go. One somewhat diversified family company we know could grow faster if the owners divested itself of its now unprofitable small string of movie theaters. The business started as a movie theater generations ago and the current owners are unable to give the theaters up because they see them as their "legacy."

Some families businesses don't grow because family members don't want their enterprises to become so large that a family member can't be CEO. In other cases, the owners are making enough money to support the family's lifestyle and don't see a need to take on the additional pressures required to expand. Still other owners simply don't want to make the sacrifices necessary to invest in people and infrastructure that are essential for growth.

One particularly good reason for not growing too large is that being small and family-owned differentiates a business from larger companies. Many family firms sell themselves to customers and employees on the notion that "you don't want to go with a large corporation that doesn't know who you are. You want to work with us, because we care about you." And, all else being equal, customers often feel better doing business with a family enterprise. "I trust it," they reason. "I think it will have higher integrity and higher

*One particularly good reason for not growing too large is that being small and family-owned differentiates a business from larger companies.*

quality. I think the family will stand behind their name because I know that they're at risk if they don't." If a family business grows too big, it may lose the personal touch and its ability to differentiate itself from the larger company down the road.

---

**EXHIBIT 2** ▓▓▓▓▓▓▓▓▓▓▓▓▓▓▓▓▓▓▓▓▓▓▓▓▓▓▓▓

## *What Owners Say About Staying Small*

1. "Being smaller and family owned is what sets our company apart from big, corporate competitors."

2. "All our family's money is tied up in this business. We cannot take large risks."

3. "If we grow, I'll have to bring in outside people to help run the business, and I just don't want to give up control. Besides, we don't want this business to become so large that a family member can't run it."

4. "We'll need outside money to expand, and we don't want to go into debt."

5. "We just don't know how to grow the business. How could we manage as many employees as growth would require?"

6. "Our grandfather started this business and we want to honor his legacy by keeping the company the way it has always been."

7. "Growth just means we'll have to pay more taxes!"

---

## The Many Meanings of Growth

When we think of business growth, we usually think of growth in terms of revenues. We want to know, "How much more did the company earn this year compared to last?" Or, "How does revenue this year compare to five years ago?"

But there are other ways to think about growth, and you, your family and senior managers may find it helpful to explore these alternatives in your own deliberations.

Increasing profitability is a very important measure of growth. A business cannot survive without profits, so many owners use profitability as the standard by which they gauge growth. Some family businesses look at profitability with a twist. They add back to profits any compensation or other benefits owners may take out of the company that are above and beyond what would be taken out under different ownership. The purpose of this is to give a clear sense of the profit generating capacity of the business. If the compensation of key non-family managers is based on profitability, it is important to consider removing extra compensation the family may take, so that managers are not discouraged by their inability to control profitability.

Another family business may measure growth in the number of employees on the payroll. One of the values of this family is to create jobs for the community in which it is located. Family businesses in very competitive markets may look at growth in terms of the market share. They may be more concerned about losing customers than about other financial measures.

DeNean Stafford uses a variety of measurements of growth for Stafford Development Company. "Cash flow is our common denominator. We look at retail and office development as a square footage business," he says, noting that the company manages and owns about 3 million square feet of retail and office space. He measures the construction equipment segment of the business by top line revenue, but he also measures growth in terms of employees, which numbered about 250 when he became CEO in 1997 and has increased to 850. Finally, he measures growth geographically. His father founded the company in south Georgia in 1947. Today it has operations throughout the southeast United States and in Ohio.

But growth means more than numbers to Stafford. "It's more of a measuring stick of success." For him, it means creating long term value, developing a new property, creating a new business, which, in turn, provides "a great opportunity for our associates so they can raise their families and enjoy what they're doing." It also provides a venue for the growth of family members. "Growth is not only numbers," he explains, "but the personal development of the members of the family and the understanding of their place in the business—whether or not they're involved in the daily management of the business."

**Grow-or-die strategies often overlook other opportunities for meaningful and positive change.**

If you choose not to grow in size, you can still grow by improving systems and processes, a requirement for businesses that want to increase revenues, profits, and all the other numerical measures. Management psychologist Edwin A. Hoover says, "Grow-or-die strategies often overlook other opportunities for meaningful and positive change."[5] Aside from growth in sales, he suggests four other growth options:

—In competence (understanding what differentiates your company and "serves as your strongest foundation for continued success").

—In strength (getting better at determining the company's best customers and suppliers and becoming more disciplined).

—In integrity (becoming more proficient at doing what you say you'll do, showing respect to stakeholders).

—In performance (providing the best customer service and responsiveness).

When you expand your definitions of growth, you may find that where once you were reluctant to adopt a growth strategy, now you are excited about doing so. If in the past, growth meant only an increase in size or numbers, you may have viewed the risks as too large to make attempting growth attractive. Now, if you think of growth as improving performance or strength or enlarging the business's ability to make a contribution to the community, you may discover a whole new world of opportunity. You will also find that thinking of growth as growing better, not bigger, is an effective way to protect your family business against the competition. But, if you are the kind of person that thinks "grow or die" means that you have to grow financially year after year, you may overlook meaningful growth opportunities that are not financial in nature.

*You will also find that thinking of growth as growing better, not bigger, is an effective way to protect your family business against the competition.*

## Healthy Conversations

Growth has implications for all the stakeholders in a family business; the owners, their successors, employees, suppliers, customers and the board. It's healthy and important for the owners, board and management to have ongoing, explicit conversations about the topic. Too often, people in family businesses don't have such conversations. A CEO might have a conversation about growth with her management team but not with the board or the ownership group. Each of these stakeholder groups should have its own discussions and carry on conversations with one another. The conversations should begin with the owners.

They need to ask, what do we want from the business as owners/investors? Their answers should be taken to their board and ultimately to management who determines whether or not their expectations of growth are reasonable and develops a plan to achieve them.

Ultimately, stakeholders need to direct their attention to three major questions:

(1) Should we grow or not?

(2) If so, how much should we grow?

(3) How will we get there?

It is important to remember that the first two questions are topics for the owners to discuss with input from their board and management. The third question, how will we get there, is for management to answer. It is then the board's responsibility to oversee management to ensure their success.

Chapters IV and V will help you address these issues and put you on the road to planned, careful, smart growth.

**EXHIBIT 3**

## *What "Growth" Means to Different Owners*

—An increase in company revenue.

—An increase in company profitability.

—Creating more jobs for the family and the community.

—Improving what we do.

—Geographic expansion.

—Being more innovative to become more competitive.

—Enhancing customer service.

—Growth in market share.

# III. The Myths About Family Business Growth

Most of us assume that growth is good, but that's not necessarily accurate. When they choose to grow, family businesses need to pursue *healthy* growth, which means growth that is sustainable and profitable. Growth though can have its dark side. Some family business owners pursue growth for the wrong reasons. They set on a course of expansion and, because they have not planned carefully enough, soon find the business is out of control.

Healthy growth requires finding a balance between growth (to keep up with the competition) and sustaining a high level of quality, service and profitability. Family businesses often learn that while they can grow quickly in the short term, they may not be able to sustain growth over a longer period. They may get ahead of themselves discovering that while they are able to double the number of customers, they are unable to maintain customer service standards or they can't manufacture enough product to meet the demands of a vastly enlarged customer base. Cash-flow problems may occur. "More people want our products than we realized," the owners say.

> *Healthy growth requires finding a balance between growth (to keep up with the competition) and sustaining a high level of quality, service and profitability.*

"Now what are we going to do?" What seemed like a great idea—growth—can lead to a host of sales, marketing, production, personnel or financial problems that can jeopardize the very continuation of the family's business legacy. One well-known brand of fast food restaurants introduced a new product that was so popular with the customers, the restaurants ran out in the first week of the promotion. Franchisees were unhappy; customers were unhappy; and marketing dollars were wasted advertising a product that couldn't be bought.

Here are three particularly popular myths surrounding business growth. Each has its own implications and requires careful thought as family business owners consider growth strategies.

## MYTH #1: GROWTH WILL MAKE US MORE PROFITABLE.

Maybe, maybe not. Happily for many business owners, growth does result in greater profits. However, growth also requires taking on more risk. For most businesses, growth necessitates looking for new customers, new geographic locations or developing new products or services. Attracting new customers or creating new products or services often requires substantial investment, exposing the company to additional risks. You may decide to discount your prices to win new customers. Discounting prices will almost inevitably reduce profit margins, stimulate competitors to match your prices and may be difficult to reverse in the long-run, once customers get used to a lower price. The old adage, "You have to spend money to make money," holds. While growth can lead to additional profits, it generally takes money—and time—to achieve. Investments may be required which provide returns only after a period of time. So, increases in the top line, which is most often what people characterize as growth, doesn't always mean growth in the bottom line. Growth often means moving out of a protected niche, getting into areas that you don't know as well and facing a new set of competitors. That could result in a bigger business with less money to show for it at the end of the day. Research has shown that family businesses tend to focus on differentiation strategies where profits are higher and they can leverage skills and experience. If there isn't room to grow in their niche, family businesses need to find other areas and people to help them achieve their new goals.

## MYTH #2: GROWTH WILL CREATE JOBS.

True—if the business grows, you usually need additional employees. But what business owners often overlook is that growth also puts a burden on existing personnel and possibly on family relationships. What if, in expanding your business, the needs of the company outgrow the talents of your current management team? You may feel loyalty toward a long-term key employee because she helped the business grow to its present level. You now recognize that she doesn't have the skills and expertise needed to take the business to the next level. Are you ready to put her out of a job or choose to promote over her? What if a family member is being bypassed? Many a family business owner has had to say, "My son's not capable of running a business this big." That's a frightening prospect. You might find that the business exceeds even your ability to manage it. Will you be able to face the possibility of bringing in a CEO from outside the family who can do a better job?

As a business expands, existing managers—including yourself—will have to delegate more responsibility to others and focus less on the daily operations and more on the long term. Family business managers who enjoy the nuts and bolts of the job and who

*As a business expands, existing managers will have to delegate more responsibility to others and focus less on the daily operations and more on the long term.*

like to "get their hands dirty" might grow themselves out of the work that gives them the most satisfaction. Their rarely chosen alternative is to keep doing what they enjoy and hire someone else to think about the bigger picture and develop strategy.

When a family business grows beyond the managerial capabilities of the next generation, family owners are faced with multiple dilemmas. Can non-family executives be identified, recruited and motivated to lead the business? Are owners, through the board of directors, prepared to provide necessary oversight and accountability? Does the family want to continue its ownership absent a family member running the company? Can family members handle the complex dynamics of dealing with such issues and reach agreement about growth, leadership, governance and ownership issues? Finding answers to these questions can take years of discussion so family businesses must be able to think well into the future, anticipating the potential implications of growth in relation to leadership issues.

Growth changes everyone's job, including that of the family owners and managers. Growth moves you out of your comfort zone. While growth will create more jobs, business owners need to think about the impact that growth will have on current employees and ask themselves, "Are we ready for this?"

*Growth moves you out of your comfort zone.*

## MYTH #3: GROWTH WILL GIVE ME MORE FREEDOM.

"If I had a bigger business, it would generate more cash and I could have time off to go play golf." Sound familiar? Many owner/managers see growth as a path to freedom and a means to enjoying hobbies, travel, or a vacation home. "If our company was larger," they think, "I could hire more employees to help me. And, I could also take more money out of the business for things that I've always wanted to do."

If healthy growth is achieved, a business owner can indeed realize his or her dream of greater freedom. But getting to that level of growth can require giving up freedom, not gaining it. It may necessitate adding debt or getting money from outside investors—and then having to report back to them. It almost always requires giving up some managerial control because you can no longer run the business by yourself. Growth means more challenges, more problems, more people, and more money. As the owner of a business that had grown from nothing to over $7 billion in sales said: "Business is just one problem after another. Fortunately, I love solving problems." If you share this philosophy, growth may be for you.

### Consider the Stress of Growth

The downsides of these myths point out that growing a business can be just as stressful as it is exhilarating. You may have to bring in outside money. You may have to risk wounding the feelings of loyal key employees if you have to bypass them in search of executives more able to run a larger operation. Growth constantly requires you to do things differently, never allowing you to rest comfortably on your accomplishments.

Several years ago, Murray Berstein, CEO of Nixon Uniform Service & Medical Wear, a growing family firm based in Wilmington, Delaware, was advised by his board to expand and reorganize his senior management team. Berstein retained his operations and finance chiefs, both of whom had been with the company for several years. His oldest son, Jason, was already fulfilling the senior marketing slot, and an executive from outside the business was hired to head sales. "I wanted to bring in someone that knew a lot more than we knew," says Berstein, adding that the sales executive "has brought a depth of extra knowledge to our company."

About a year and a half later, the chief operating officer gave notice he was quitting. "I think he resigned because at one time, he ran almost the whole company except finance," says Berstein. Now he had two additional peers to work with—the marketing and sales executives—and Berstein felt that the COO did not like the idea of these additional executives being his equal nor having to face the challenge they represented. And, Berstein adds, "Because of the growth, it's a very pressured environment here, and he just didn't want the pressure anymore."

**Growth is not just stressful for the owner, managers and employees. It's also stressful for the whole family system.** Consider the founder of a business who, in the early years, doesn't have as much time as he wanted to spend with his children. He tells himself that eventually, "I'm going to be able to give back that time that I lost with my family." But if he keeps growing the business, without adequate support, he won't have the time to give back. He thinks things will get better and he'll have more time for the family but it doesn't happen. In time, his family begins to feel resentment because he spends so little time with them.

Consider the son who has been told by his dad that the business has outdistanced the younger man's ability to run it. Not only does he feel the stress of being rejected (no matter how compassionate his father was in breaking the news) but now the stress is passed on to his wife and perhaps to his children, who are, after all, the next generation of the family and the family business.

There are no easy answers here, just things to consider.

## Facing the Fears

Lest these cautions seem too discouraging, keep in mind that **many family business owners look at these issues, face their fears, and embrace growth anyway, with good results.** Berstein has aimed at growth that would double the business every four to five years and so far, he has been successful. "Our company benefits by being larger because of the quality of staff we're able to attract and the purchasing power you have when it's bigger." And, he added, "The environment's more professional." Besides, Berstein likes the business he's in and sees the competition as a game. "I just like to see the accomplishment of our business savvy, and growth is one of the tools [by which] we can measure accomplishment."

What's more, according to Berstein, growth has made his life not only different but easier. The people he has hired to run the different aspects of his company, he says, "have more ability in those areas than I probably ever had."

The key is to think about growth with your eyes open, understanding the upside and downside of growth, so that you can make an informed decision and appropriate plans about what is right for you, your family and the family business.

# IV. "How Much Growth Is Right for Our Business?"

*Deciding how much to grow means taking an honest, objective look at whether or not the business is capable of the growth required to meet the objectives set forth.*

Suppose you and the other owners of your company have looked at all the questions and issues raised in the last two chapters. You've explored the pros and cons of growth with your senior managers, board of directors, and key family members, including potential owners and successors (if they are adults). Together, you have decided that you want the business to grow and you've come to an agreement on what growth means. Now you are ready to spend some serious time answering the second question posed at the end of Chapter II: "How much should we grow?"

It's not enough to just throw out some figure, like "We want to grow by 20 percent a year," or, "We need to double our business every five years." **Deciding how much to grow means determining what you want from the business.** It also means taking an honest, objective look at whether or not the business is capable of the growth required to meet the objectives set forth.

## Why Do We Want To Grow?

A good place to begin determining whether growth is right for you is to think about what's behind your desire to grow. What do you and other family members want from the business? What is the purpose of growth? To stay competitive? To enable Mom and Dad to retire in

*What is the purpose of growth?*

five years? To create senior management jobs for three siblings? To pay family members in the business more money? To award higher dividends to shareholders? To meet the new demands of customers? To provide more jobs for family members or others? Do you want to expand into a new field of business because that's what your sons are passionate about? These are many of the typical reasons families' state as to why they want to grow their businesses, and you will probably come up with additional reasons of your own. **It will help to avoid taking an attitude of "growth for growth's sake" and to think instead of growth as a means to an end, not an end itself.**

You will also need to define what you mean by growth. As you will recall from Chapter II, family business owners view growth in many different ways. Are you talking about top-line growth? Growth in the number of customers or employees? Growth in market share? In the end, your business will only be successful if it makes money, so it's important that the way you define growth translates into profits.

Keep in mind that **it's the owner's responsibility to decide what the business' needs and goals are. The owners need to say as a unified group, "This is OUR investment," and we should not abdicate these important decisions to the CEO, management team or even to the owners working in the business. Owners not involved in the daily operations have a voice too.** Since growth is not easy to achieve, owners will want to think carefully about their rationale for growth, asking such questions as, "Do we really need to double the business in five years to support family members? Are there other avenues we could pursue to ensure that everyone is taken care of?"

Don't be surprised if your discussions unearth competing objectives. Dad's reasonable and well-earned desire to retire and take money out of the company may conflict with his daughter's understandable wish to re-invest profits for future opportunities. Some shareholders' longing for higher dividends may be at odds with the CEO's hopes of providing better benefits for the employees. The family's desire to create more jobs for the community may conflict with the reality that the community is too small and remote to attract good senior managers. Some family members may want to sell the company while others hope it will be passed on to the next generation. What's important is that all the shareowners' have the opportunity to express their desires. For more information about ownership, you may want to read *Family Business Ownership: How to Be an Effective Shareholder* by Craig E. Aronoff and John L. Ward.

## Is the Business Capable?

As you consider what the family wants from the business, it will be just as important to assess what the business can actually achieve. Can it truly sustain the growth needed to satisfy a given objective or a combination of goals? If not, can you bring the business to the point where it can support the growth you want? Or will you have to adopt a less ambitious growth plan and curtail your objectives? The next two chapters will provide you with some tools to assess your growth capability.

But for now, understand that in your discussions, you will keep going back and forth between these questions—"What do we want from the business?" and "Can it support the growth needed to meet our objectives? If not, can we make it ready?" Eventually, you will arrive at a realistic understanding of how much growth is right for you, what its objectives are, what kind of growth it is, and how you are going to achieve it.

Expect some disagreement. That's normal. If Dad wants to retire and figured out that it's not in his best interest to build another plant because he needs to withdraw money from the company, he'll opt for holding steady. If he makes a good case, his daughter and other shareholders will understand and say, "Maybe we should be focusing on profits right now, not growth."

In some cases, when an analysis of a business shows that it is not capable of the growth needed to meet the family's objectives, the family may decide to go into a different business altogether. The Stafford Development Company mentioned earlier started out as an automobile and farm equipment dealership more than 50 years ago. But it now has interests in the hospitality industry, retail development and management, real estate, and restaurants.

*Understand that in your discussions, you will keep going back and forth between these questions—"What do we want from the business?" and "Can it support the growth needed to meet our objectives? If not, can we make it ready?"*

## Facilitating the Dialogue

You'll need a forum for your conversations about growth. If all the owners are on the board, board meetings will be the likely venue. DeNean Stafford and his two sisters, Mary Jane Theden and Sally Stafford Perez own Stafford Development equally and, while the sisters are not active in the company's day-to-day operations, they serve on its board (along with three outside directors) and hold leadership roles in the Stafford family council. According to DeNean Stafford, they work hard at their directors' roles, listening to all the sides of the issues on which they need to decide. "They might have misgivings about a particular decision. They might have some questions. They might be apprehensive. But a little bit of that's probably normal," says Stafford. He makes sure that his sisters are provided with as much information as possible, filling them in on what management wants to do and why and how it expects to go about it. "The outside directors have given them a comfort level and the board added expertise," says Stafford.

For many family businesses, family meetings will be the most appropriate place for such conversations. If your family does not already hold such meetings, it's a good idea to start. Two books helpful in the planning and execution of family meetings are, *Family Meetings: How to Build a Stronger Family and a Stronger Business*, and *Family Business Governance: Maximizing Family and Business Potential*.

Whatever you do, have the conversations and have them to completion. Don't stop at "What do we want from this business?" Have the second part of the dialogue as well—the honest appraisal of the company's ability to grow and support your objectives. If needed, invite your management to advise you on the company's abilities. Too many families have the first discussion but skip the second. The entrepreneur generation of the business often makes decisions intuitively rather than being data driven. They may bring tremendous industry exposure to the table and think that the data is not relevant. They also may not have formal training to assess growth opportunities.

## Avoid Speed Traps

As you set your growth objectives, don't be dazzled by fast growth. Growing too fast is often the road to ruin. Controlled, manageable growth is what you want. Stafford observes that while the growth at Stafford Development has been substantial, "It's been done over quite a period of time, and it's been methodical." In his view, the pace of the growth has minimized the risk placed on the company.

*Controlled, manageable growth is what you want.*

One business owner told *Nation's Business* magazine that when other owners tell him they grew 45 percent in one year, he commiserates with them. He knows how stressful it is to grow that swiftly and finds himself satisfied with growth at a more controllable rate of 15 to 25 percent. "Growth manages you if you let it," he said. "The challenge is to manage the growth."[6]

Family-owned and managed Blue Bell Creameries has developed the third largest ice cream brand in the United States. With over $400 million in sales, it distributes in only fourteen states. The Kruse family has preferred slow, controlled growth since the business's founding in 1919. They even have a slogan for it: "It's a cinch by the inch." Another example of managed growth is Chick-fil-A, a fast food chain of chicken restaurants. Founded in Georgia, it remained in the southeast for years before expanding into additional states. Chick-fil-A does not franchise, preferring to own all units even if it takes a longer time period to grow.

# V. Where Does Growth Come From?

The family-owned grocery chain, Wegmans Food Markets, Inc., has grown to more than $3 billion in sales in recent years. Founded in 1916 and based in Rochester, New York, the company has aggressively pursued geographic expansion and now numbers around 70 stores in four states and is soon to enter a fifth.

In Harleysville, Pennsylvania, Sherry S. Russell, president of Alderfer Inc., a meat company started by her grandfather in 1922, has been pursuing growth by a different route—acquiring two nearby family-owned meat companies. "This is not the norm for Alderfer's," she said. "Alderfer's has never acquired a company, and now all of a sudden we're acquiring two companies at once."[7] At the time of the acquisitions, the purchases would double Alderfer's size to 140 employees and annuals sales to $40 million.

Another Pennsylvania family-owned company, Emmaus-based publisher Rodale Inc., has achieved remarkable growth in recent years in large part because it has been so innovative. Once known for its *Organic Farming and Gardening* (now *Organic Gardening*) and *Prevention* magazines, the company expanded its concept of health publishing to include active living, fitness, spirituality and nature. Under Steve Murphy, a non-family CEO hired in 2000, Rodale's profits nearly doubled from 2002 to 2004 with the introduction of the phenomenally best-selling book, *The South Beach Diet*, as well as two new magazines, *Best Life* and *Women's Health*.[8]

As these three companies suggest, there are many ways to achieve growth in a family business. Where will growth come from for your company? The key to remember is that **growth is driven by opportunities, so you need to look for what opportunities are out there for you**. A valuable tool in planning for growth is The Growth Matrix below. It can help you determine what your company is capable of and how you are most likely to achieve it.

*...there are many ways to achieve growth in a family business.*

Once you have set a growth goal, you will need to figure out where that growth is coming from. The first step is to outline what growth you can expect if you continue to do things the way you always have. (You may need to acknowledge that doing things the same way could actually cause you to shrink rather than grow.) You will need data that tells you how much business you gain and lose each year, as well as information on trends in the marketplace, to figure out what growth you'll have by maintaining the status quo. You don't need to have perfect numbers. What's important is to be directionally correct.

Once you have this base, you can calculate what you need to reach your goal. Then, you need to figure out how you will make up the difference.

EXHIBIT 4 ████████████████████████████████

# THE GROWTH MATRIX

| | Same | New |
|---|---|---|
| **New** | • Develop new product extensions for existing customers | • Reinvent the business, offering new products and services to new customers |
| **Same** | • Improve customer retention<br><br>• Take market share from competitors<br><br>• Take advantage of market growth | • Identify other customers/market segments to buy existing products |

*New* (top left) ... *Same* (bottom left)

PRODUCTS

Same — New

**CUSTOMER MARKETS**

## Start With Existing Customers

Most people start by thinking about the bottom left quadrant of the Matrix, selling the same products and services to the same customer markets. This does not mean the exact same customers. If you are running a retail laundry service and new customers who live around the corner from your store come in, they represent the same customer market. But, if you went to a local gym and offered to launder its towels, a market segment not yet served by a family business, this would represent a new customer market.

There are three ways to achieve growth with existing customer markets:

—Improve customer retention.

—Acquire market share from competitors.

—Take advantage of market growth.

By far the least expensive and most effective method is improving customer retention. If you lose a customer, consider how much effort and time it will take to replace him. If you are counting on a certain amount of growth coming from new customers, how much time and effort will it take to win them? How many different potential customers do you have to call

22

on to get one customer to buy? Business owners frequently say, "I have to call on five people before I get one new customer." If that's the case with your business and your goal is to secure 20 new customers of a given size in the coming year that means you have to call on 100 potential clients. Business owners often tell me that from the time they first call on a potential buyer to the time that individual actually places an order will take six months. In many businesses, it takes a considerable amount of time to prospect new customers before you are able to start realizing your projected growth.

It may be wiser to focus on the customers you already have. If you run a restaurant, could you sell more to each person who comes in? ("How about a salad with your burger?" Or, "Can I interest you in dessert?") Can you entice them to come in more often? ("We're now offering a breakfast special. Give it a try on your way to work.") A local delicatessen now stocks casseroles by their cash register. They are not open during the dinner hour but those eating at the deli at lunchtime can purchase dinner to take home. Can you find ways to encourage them to bring others? (Think of children's' birthday parties and end-of-the-season celebrations for sports teams.)

Focusing on customer retention also means finding out why you are losing customers and then doing something about it. Murray Berstein at Nixon Uniform Service & Medical Wear became alarmed not long ago when his company's lost-business-numbers were higher than in the past. "It's more costly to replace lost customers, and financially, we felt it," says Berstein. With existing customers, for example, you have to provide new uniforms only when they need replacement. With new customers, however, you have more sales expense and you have to buy all new uniforms for the customers' employees.

An analysis by an outside firm showed a decline in customer service, particularly a lack of speed in returning customer phone calls. Berstein realized that the executive who had been put in charge of customer service was not suited to the job and that the customer service staff was not living up to the company's mission "to provide the highest standard of textile rental service to customers who appreciate the best." Staffing changes were made and Nixon's customer service was soon back on track, returning customer calls immediately and visiting customers when necessary. "We treated them the way they deserved to be treated," says Berstein. "Every customer is important."

Another facet of customer retention is turning "bad" customers into good ones. Bad customers may be those who always pay late or whose purchases are so minimal that you lose money trying to serve them. They may be demanding customers that take up so much time and attention that you lose money on them instead of making a profit. Some business owners find that at times they have to stop doing business with bad customers and concentrate on the good ones. Before you do, try to find a way of converting them, providing discounts as incentives to people who pay bills early, or offering an attractive mass produced item instead of a custom-made one at a price that's much less expensive but still very profitable for you.

Sometimes people think of growth as "more and new." They ignore the fact that research shows that it's easier to sell to people who already know you than to people who don't. Moreover, it makes much more sense to try to keep the customers you have and figure out what else they need that you could provide. That's an easier way to grow.

Some business owners believe the easiest way to grow is by expanding their market share. That means selling products and services they know to customers they understand. However, increasing market share means taking customers from competitors—a challenge if your rivals are strong. Growth from increased market shares may require lower prices (which can hurt your profits) or investing in ways to differentiate yourself from the competition.

One trick is to try to estimate your share of customers' purchases. You look at what they buy from you, but you may rarely think about what they buy from someone else. You probably have some instincts about this, but a simple customer questionnaire might turn up useful information. Do you have 100 percent of your customers' business? If not, what would you need to do to get it? What you want to do is capture more of your existing customers' business. Will that mean lowering prices? Offering more products and services? Providing such incentives as frequent buyers' programs? Improving service or being friendlier?

*Do you have 100 percent of your customers' business?*

Taking competitors' customers is difficult to do, and your competitors will work to keep them. You have to be able to offer something more valuable than your competitors do or people won't switch. Smart competitors will build in "costs" to keep customers from switching vendors. A "switching cost" is the cost to the customer of doing business with someone else. It can be monetary, emotional, or a matter of convenience. If you as a customer switch from one airline to another, you might lose the benefit of your frequent-flier miles. If you switch your life insurance carrier, you might have to go through the inconvenience of another physical exam. Some customers will continue to do business with you because they can say, "I know the owner." They would miss that personal touch if they went to that chain restaurant or big-box store down the street, and that loss would be a switching cost for them.

The third way to grow by selling the same products and services to the same customer markets is by taking advantage of market growth. If you compete in a growing market, you can often grow without taking customers from anyone. In fact, if a market is growing fast enough, you can grow revenues while losing market share. It pays to focus your attention on markets that are growing and less on markets that are not. Rodale demonstrated that concept over the years by focusing less on the dwindling farming market and more on the growing numbers of readers who wanted to know about organic gardening and healthy eating and living.

Wegmans Food Markets, in its geographic expansion, has taken market share from competitors and taken advantage of market growth. A good example is the opening of its store in Downingtown, Pennsylvania. Not only was it a threat to the local Giant, part of the Netherlands-based international food company, Ahold, but it also posed a challenge to smaller, local family-owned companies. Giant responded by moving its nearest store to much larger and cleaner-looking quarters, lowering prices, offering many more items, and adding new departments, including a take-out café. Clemens Markets Inc., a local family-owned grocer, closed the store nearest the Wegmans location and enlarged and revamped stores a bit further away.

In entering Downingtown as in entering other communities, Wegmans also took advantage of market growth. Three new townhouse communities are being developed within two miles of the new store. All represent new families and households who need the goods—from pet food and laundry detergent to truffles and sushi—that the inventive Wegmans can supply.

## New Sources of Growth

You can go through a similar analysis with each of the other quadrants in The Growth Matrix. For new products and services, you can ask yourself such questions as: What are our customers buying from someone else that they could be buying from us? Are there logical add-on products we could offer to help meet our customers' needs? Rodale is a good example of a family firm that has been very skillful in developing new product extensions for existing customers. Capitalizing on the wild success of *The South Beach Diet*, for example, Rodale followed with *The South Beach Diet Good Fats, Good Carbs Guide* and *The South Beach Diet Cookbook*.

**Remember that any new products and services you come up with must be within your capability to deliver.** Many businesses fail trying to provide new offerings that they don't have the capacity to produce. If you can't provide a competitive offering, trying to do so is not the right path for growth.

When considering new customer markets, think about who else might value what you do. New markets can mean expanding geographically, as Wegmans has done, but they can also mean looking at new customer segments. Nixon Uniform Service started in 1967 as a dry-cleaning business and soon evolved into renting and cleaning industrial uniforms. Over time, it was providing not just uniforms but mats, towels, and other textiles for car dealers, spas and beauty salons, and food service businesses. Nixon identified another market segment in the medical community, supplying lab coats, scrubs, patient gowns, and linens to doctors' offices and hospitals. The beauty of serving this new set of customers was twofold: Nixon could use the infrastructure it already had, and none of Nixon's competitors were really focusing on this niche.

If you are contemplating going into either new customer markets or new products and services, it's important to consider the level of existing competition in these areas. If these markets are highly competitive, it's wise to steer clear unless you are confident that you can provide something substantially better or unique than what is already available. In general, markets that are growing rapidly are less competitive than those that are stagnant, so be sure to investigate the level of growth in the new markets or products you are considering.

The toughest way to grow is found in the upper right quadrant of the Matrix, where you are offering new products to new customers. This avenue is recommended only when other approaches are unable to meet your growth expectations. This strategy can require significant capital investment and take a long time to achieve.

*If you pursue opportunities away from your primary area of expertise, bring in someone knowledgeable with the area to help you achieve success.*

The more closely the new products and markets resemble your existing business, the more likely you are to be successful. Many family businesses like to diversify into completely new areas to spread their risk. However, if your employees lack the skills or experience in a given field, your likelihood of success is low. If you pursue opportunities away from your primary area of expertise, bring in someone knowledgeable with the area to help you achieve success.

All the methods of growth we've been discussing represent growth from within a company. The best growth often comes internally. However, you can buy growth by buying another business, as Alderfer Inc., the meat company mentioned at the beginning of this chapter, has done. Alderfer's chances of succeeding with its acquisitions are reasonably good because the family is purchasing businesses it understands and it understands the customers of those new businesses. Additionally, both acquisitions are located nearby.

But remember, acquisitions often come at a steep price. There is always a premium paid to acquire customers. If you are considering an acquisition, the question you have to ask is "Will it cost less to acquire a customer through the purchase than it would cost to gain the customer on your own by taking him from the competition."

Beyond this test, **you need to consider your ability to integrate an**

**existing business into your own**. This task is difficult, particularly for companies that don't do it often. In addition, family businesses tend to have strong cultures, which can make integration more challenging.

As successful as their companies are, both DeNean Stafford at Stafford Development and Murray Berstein at Nixon Uniform Service say their companies ran into trouble with acquisitions. Nixon once acquired a company that focused largely on the distribution of such safety items as work gloves, hardhat liners, goggles, and the like. It was a mistake for several reasons, Berstein says. "One was that we didn't understand the whole business." It also didn't have the right people to manage it and, because it was a few hours away from headquarters, he says, "we just weren't there enough. It wasn't the main core of our thought process." Eventually, Nixon sold off the safety-supply portion of the acquisition.

DeNean Stafford says that trying to double the size of Stafford's foods company by acquiring a 15-store Wendy's franchise operation in South Florida was "probably the worst mistake we ever made." Stafford Development had thought it could duplicate in South Florida what it had done successfully with its Wendy's restaurants in South Georgia. However, it found that South Florida was unlike South Georgia. "The labor pool is vastly different. Your costs of doing business are much higher as well," says DeNean Stafford. The franchise was finally sold.

## When Things Don't Add Up

Sometimes you and your management team find that the numbers don't seem to add up. You've evaluated the sources of growth suggested in this chapter and you just can't see how you're going to get where you want to go in terms of growth. However, at the end of the exercise, instead of saying, "This won't work," you need to be asking, "What could we do?" This is the time to get creative.

An excellent way to do that is to understand the strengths of the people around you—in the business, in the family, and on your board. The son of one business owner wasn't particularly good at sales, but he's great at comprehending the profitability of the company's customers. His ideas have been invaluable in helping the company to grow. Other family business leaders find that an outside board of directors helps identify opportunities that the owning families might not see.

While this book has counseled staying close to what you know, it's also important not to be overly bound by a sense of "legacy." Some families get stuck in the idea that Grandfather would want the company to stay in the business that it was in when he founded it. But what if that business was typewriter manufacturing? What subsequent generations often forget is that the founder most likely tried many things before he hit on a business idea that finally succeeded.

What happens when you try something new and it doesn't work? You try something else. It's not unusual to hear a family business owner say:

"We've done a lot of things that didn't work. But we've done one or two more good things that did. **When you make a mistake, you have to step back and cut your losses and move on.**"

## Leverage Your Advantages

Analyzing your company's ability to get where you want it to go and figuring out how to get there take discipline and a willingness to be systematic. If analysis isn't your strong suit, look around for someone in your family or in the company who thrives on it.

*You must also ask—and answer—whether or not the business is capable of the growth you want.*

Family business owners really understand their businesses. Most can pull theirs apart and tell you what's going to happen. But often they don't want to do that because they know or fear that things won't add up they way they want them to. Nevertheless, doing the analysis—or having a capable person do it for you—is essential. Only if you know for sure that things don't add up can you do something about it.

As we discussed in the last chapter, it's not enough to just ask: "How much growth is right for us?" You must also ask—and answer—whether or not the business is capable of the growth you want.

As you seek to answer these questions, remember that family businesses have a number of special strengths that can contribute to growth. One is that they tend to know their customers better than non-family companies do, and they are more relationship oriented.

Customers love to do business with family firms because they feel certain that a family company will stand behind its name. Customers also tend to believe that they and the family owners are members of the same community and that, as a result, the owners will be more supportive of the customers. Customers also may feel that there is more stability with a family company and that a family firm gives them more personalized service. One new customer recalls with pleasure how, when she called a family-owned insurance company to set a time to pick up some documents, the owner said, "We really all want to meet you. This is a small enough office that we'll all have a chance to say hello."

*...family firms can be much more flexible than other businesses.*

Another customer found himself impressed and delighted with his new family-owned accounting firm. After the customer's taxes were prepared, the 80-year-old founder, no longer active in accounting but now a good-will ambassador, sat down with the client to make sure he understood what had been done and to tell him how much his business was appreciated.

Another advantage of family firms is that, unless

they are hung up on the notion of "legacy," they can be much more flexible than other businesses. Larger, non-family companies often have to go through layers of bureaucracy and get many people to agree before change can be accomplished. A family business is more likely to have a relatively small set of owners, and if someone wants to try something new as a means to achieve growth, the owners can quickly come to agreement and give the go-ahead.

**The secret to growth with many family companies is leverage.** They leverage the strengths that characterize family firms, and instead of jumping totally into businesses they're not familiar with, they leverage what they are good at, building on their knowledge and experience.

*...family firms leverage what they are good at, building on their knowledge and experience.*

# VI. Roadblocks to Growth

Once you are comfortable that there are viable avenues for achieving the growth you want, you are halfway to your goal. Even when the opportunities exist, however, you may find that in your business, there are some roadblocks to growth that need to be addressed and overcome. The most typical obstructions are people, infrastructure, capital, and culture.

> *The most typical obstructions are people, infrastructure, capital, and culture.*

## People

If your company is to expand, you need to have people with the time and energy to pursue growth options. When I work with business owners on strategic planning, I often find that they come up with many great ideas but no one in the company has the time to execute them. It's a problem of human capacity: not enough people and not enough time.

The second people problem is lack of skills. In terms of numbers, you may have enough people, but do they have the skills and experience necessary to grow your company? This can certainly be a problem at the management level. Growing a business requires managers to move their focus from day-to-day execution to longer-term planning. Do your managers (including yourself) have the ability to identify, train and coach good people; delegate responsibility; track performance, and think strategically? All these skills are important in a growth environment.

The most challenging portion of growing a business is having the right people in the right positions, able to take the business to the next level.

Running a $10 million-a-year business is very different from running a $2 million business, and running a $100 million business is not at all like running a $10 million business. Each level of growth poses its own management challenges, and many a business owning family has found that the long-time, loyal employee who helped take the company to $10 million doesn't have the ability to take it to $50 million or $100 million. Or the business owner herself may be someone who took the company to $25 million but lacks the wherewithal to grow it further. Many businesses find that when they reach a certain size, it's no longer sufficient to have just a bookkeeper. Instead, they need to hire a chief financial officer if they are to move forward. In addition to developing or hiring employees who can manage a larger enterprise, many CEOs find that it's also essential to create an outside board of directors, with independent, knowledgeable senior executives from other companies. Many businesses also err by keeping the same law or accounting firm. Reevaluating your needs from these service providers as you grow is important. **If you have the right advisors, they will help you grow; if not, they may keep you from achieving your growth goals.**

Another change is in the professionalization of "people" management. As your company grew, an assistant (or a spouse) probably handled personnel functions. A growing company, however, may require hiring a human resources professional to develop: standards and procedures for hiring, promotions and dismissals; job descriptions; standards for pay and benefits; other personnel policies; compliance with government regulation and more.

Family business owners often struggle with their own role as it pertains to growth. They love getting into the details, knowing everything that's going on in their company. They have trouble relinquishing control of the daily operations to others and moving on to more strategic considerations. But, there is only so much one person can do. When a business owner says the reason he doesn't delegate is that he doesn't have people who can take on the responsibility, that's a cause for concern. Either he is not doing a good job of finding the right people and training them, or he is really not ready to give up some control.

"If I have a strength, it would probably be being able to hire really good people," says DeNean Stafford. When told he has a reputation for being committed to hiring people that he considers smarter than himself, he laughs heartily. "That's not really hard to do. I don't have to look very far to accomplish that."

It's not known yet if the third generation of Staffords will join the business. As this book goes to press, they are all under twenty-one years old. If he were no longer able to run the company and no one in the third generation was available, would Stafford consider having a non-family CEO? "Yeah. In a minute," he replies. "That could very well be the best way to run this company. If the next generation really wants to rise to the occasion, that's one thing. But if they want to maintain a shareholder status, I think an outside CEO would work well."

Other people issues include: What can you do about that loyal employee who is not capable of helping you take the company to the next level? Are your children getting the experience and gaining the skills they need to grow the business? What about the son or daughter who is clearly not cut out to be the leader of a growing company? Can you gently and compassionately find other roles for people who stand in the way of your company's growth, or encourage them to pursue careers elsewhere? If growth is outstripping your own abilities, can you find an executive coach who can help you learn the skills you lack? Or, can you step aside and hire someone more capable to run the company if that's what's needed?

In the face of such difficult questions, **business owners need to think hard about how important growth is to them. If you are not ready to make the trade-offs required, then growth may not be as important to you as you think.**

EXHIBIT 5

## *People Obstruct Business Growth When...*

...they don't have the capacity, time, or energy to execute good ideas.

...they lack the skills and experience essential to lead a company at the next level.

...they are CEOs or senior managers who have difficulty letting go of day-to-day operations and moving on to strategic tasks.

...resist change.

---

## Infrastructure

Many businesses are able to grow successfully for several years and then, no matter what they do, they reach a plateau. Why does this happen? Because at a certain point, businesses cannot grow any further by doing things the way they have always been done. Once this happens, it is time to "professionalize" the business.

Professionalization is different for every business. In general, it means you develop routine systems and processes that ensure consistency in the way you run your operations. For example, you can't rely on identifying billing problems by having customers calling you to register complaints when their bills are wrong. You need a system to ensure that invoices are accurate and go out in a timely fashion.

The word "system" often scares people because they think it means installing costly technology. It can mean that, but not necessarily. It simply suggests a routinized process that is followed to accomplish a standard task. When systems and standards are put in place, you can accomplish more work with fewer resources, and the quality of your work improves.

Businesses that have **not** developed systems and processes find that growing beyond a certain point is too complex. They simply cannot take on another customer or sell another product and provide excellence. Once systems are established, customers and products can be added in a way that does not require significant time or cause errors in their integration.

It's not possible to state a specific size or time at which your business will need to make an investment in developing processes, but you will know when the time comes. Warning signs include an increase

> *When systems and standards are put in place, you can accomplish more work with fewer resources, and the quality of your work improves.*

in lost business, in billing errors, or an escalation of personnel turnover. You may hit this point multiple times as you grow. Each time you take your business to the next level, it will require more and more investment.

**It's important to understand that when you make the investments needed in infrastructure that will support a substantially larger business, your profitability in the short run will generally decrease.** You may need a new plant, a better computer system, or high-level employees (such as chief financial officer, a chief operating officer, a vice president of human resources, or a plant manager). In most cases, short-term growth will not cover the cost of these investments. Additionally, and as important, there is the investment of time. Documenting key processes in the business, developing standards for them, and training employees to follow them all take time. So, in the short term, the business may see a reduction rather than an increase in productivity. Fortunately, family businesses have a reputation for investing for the long term and not for immediate returns.

> *...family businesses have a reputation for investing for the long term and not for immediate returns.*

Keep in mind that yours is not the first business to reach this point. There's plenty of help available to you so take advantage of it. If a "friendly competitor" invites you on a plant tour to see how they do things, accept the invitation. If your industry association prints benchmarks in certain areas, compare yourself to them and analyze your strengths and weaknesses.

Professionalizing is troublesome for many family firms because the family members in management may not have worked anywhere else; and don't have a model of how to do things differently. They can therefore be reluctant to change what has worked for them so far. Because they are hesitant about sharing information, they frequently won't work with industry associations to learn other ways of doing things. Board members who have grown a business of your size to the next level can advise management on how to institute the changes needed.

A particular challenge occurs when the successor generation recognizes the need to professionalize but the generation running the business does not. It may be difficult for the next generation to convince their parents that areas need to be changed. A book in the Family Business Leadership Series that can be helpful in this case is *Make Change Your Family Business Tradition*.

### Financing Growth

Financing growth can be a roadblock when a business-owning family lacks sufficient access to capital or simply does not wish to take on debt. Some families are most insistent about never borrowing money—"Grandpa never did, Dad never did, and we're not going to borrow money either."

Nevertheless, **growth needs the fuel that capital provides**. Business owners need to ask such questions as: What is it going to take financially to grow this company? Are we willing to take out a loan to build a new plant or buy the fleet of trucks? If we're not, are there ways to generate capital internally or should we scale back on our aspirations?

Another consideration is ROIC—return on invested capital. When you have dollars invested in your family company, you have to think of more than just profit margins; you have to be mindful of the return on your investment as well. Suppose that for every $10 of sales, you get $1 back after expenses. That's a 10% profit margin. But suppose you have to invest $200,000 in a new machine for your facility. It will take 20,000 sales at $10 each (with $1 profit) before you even begin to realize a return on your investment. This is a vastly simplified example, of course, but you get the picture. Even if growth is profitable, it may yield a low return on your investment. You need to look at both profit and investment when considering whether growth makes sense.

If financing is a stumbling block, it makes sense to consider incremental growth. "Hit many singles and doubles, not just home runs," is the advice of renowned management consultant Ram Charan. In his book, *Profitable Growth Is Everyone's Business*, he says, "While home runs provide the opportunity for a quantum increase in the growth trajectory, they are unpredictable and don't happen all the time. Singles and doubles, however, can happen every day of the year. They result from a determined, day-in and day-out improvement in the activities…of a company."[9]

Here's another perspective on financing growth:

# Reducing the Risks of Family-Business Growth

By Joseph H. Astrachan

We've heard financial strategies in family businesses expressed in many ways, ranging from "I just want to get out of debt" to "I'll take every dollar anyone will lend me." Our experience suggests that more family businesses would make the first statement; they don't like debt and the risks that it causes.

Unwillingness to use debt, however, can restrict a company's ability to grow. Professionals in corporate finance develop strategies that blend debt and equity to maximize return on investment and support business growth. Our research has shown that companies with debt expect more and faster growth than do those without debt.

We do not suggest that every family business should run out and borrow money for growth. But in a recent survey, over half of business owners said they feel they have excellent access to capital. Besides capital, growth requires market opportunities, managerial ability to take advantage of opportunity, and the desire and motivation to grow.

In our experience, family business owners realize that growth, debt, and risk can further complicate family relationships. Aggressive growth strategies require more-sophisticated management practices and better communication with family owners. Communication, management controls, and accountability help reduce risk from growth and greatly reduce stress and perceptions of undue risk among family members.

In analyzing data, we found that old, multiple-generation family businesses tend to have three things in common: a strategic plan, a board of directors, and family meetings. Each of these characteristics seems to be associated with business growth and the ability to manage growth and economic downturns well.

Growth, particularly rapid growth, requires strategic planning. Families that are conflicted over business direction become much more supportive when management develops and expresses a clear direction and a plan to get there.

For family businesses embarking on growth strategies that require greater risk, having an active board of directors becomes even more important. Boards can provide oversight, ideas, and experience to help companies manage risk responsibly.

Our research shows that three-fourths of businesses that hold regular family meetings expect significant growth, compared with 60 percent of those that do not meet. Family meetings are an important way to build consensus for growth.

Here are some things we believe growing family businesses should do in their family meetings:

—Clarify family goals. Discuss how business growth can help achieve those goals. Examples include providing employment opportunities for more family members, remaining competitive in a changing industry, and building wealth.

—Make sure that the family understands the use of debt in business. Talk about corporate-finance concepts, principles, and ratios.

—Develop clear policies on debt levels, expected return on investment, and rewards to owners. The family should understand that business leaders are taking a responsible and disciplined approach to risk and that family owners can expect rewards for the risks they are asked to assume.

—Share financial reports with family owners on a regular basis—at the end of each quarter often makes sense. Emphasize results, of course, but also discuss key ratios that indicate how well risk is being managed.

—Discuss estate plans with the family. Careful planning is required to assure that the benefits of risk and growth remain with the business and the family. Unless estate planning is accomplished and understood, growth will simply cause estate taxes to be higher and harder to pay.

---

## Culture

A company's culture can be a detriment to growth if it is bureaucratic, "smothering innovation, substituting rules for common sense, stultifying decision-making, and straitjacketing initiative," warns Donald K. Clifford, Jr., and Richard E. Cavanagh in their book, *The Winning Performance*, a report on high-growth, mid-size companies. The good news, in my experience, is that family businesses tend not to be bureaucratic. Instead, their leaders generally resemble the CEOs of the "winning companies" that Clifford and Cavanagh studied. These researchers expected the CEOs of high-growth companies to talk about themselves in interviews and meetings. Instead, most of them "talked about corporate credos and philosophies—literate, concise statements of values. In each case, these credos vividly set forth the company's guiding principles; defining the ways value is to be created for customers, the rights and responsibilities of employees, and, most important, an overall affirmation of 'what we stand for.'"[10]

They found that such credos were one of the most "powerful weapons" in these high-performing companies. As they point out, however, credos were more than words. They were passionately held beliefs reflected in company action.

> *A culture that doesn't encourage taking a hard look at yourself, comparing your business to your competitors and other benchmarks in your industry will stultify your company's growth.*

Family business owners frequently speak with excitement about their family and business values and what their company stands for. Some have written mission statements that are shared with employees and customers. Perhaps you have done so, too. However, if you find your company exhibiting some of the negative signals we talked about, such as more lost business or employee turnover, it may be wise to take a look at your company culture and determine if it is having a deleterious effect on your ability to grow. One of the ways that the family business culture can impede growth is the "not invented here" syndrome. I often hear, "We've always done it this way; or my grandfather did it that way so it's good enough for us." A culture that doesn't encourage taking a hard look at yourself, comparing your business to your competitors and other benchmarks in your industry will stultify your company's growth. A family business we know that had successful growth had two slogans. One was "Double It" referring to the company's sales which it sought to double every four years. Their other slogan referred to all aspects of the business and supported their sales goal. "Find a Better Way," is always said and that's exactly what they did—all the time.

# VII. Managing Diverse Expectations

By now it's clear that, as the business's leader, you have a number of stakeholder groups to manage in a family firm: owners, managers, other employees, and the family itself. You will find it much more difficult to achieve growth if these groups are not aligned in their desire to see the business expand.

## Owner Differences

Anticipate diverging perspectives. Within the family, there will be differences that pose potential problems. Family owners who work in the business may be much more interested in growth than those not in the business, who may prefer to take money out rather than re-invest it. Those in the business are more likely to see the opportunities for growth. "I think we could make a lot of money doing this," one of them might say. But those outside the business will not have the same confidence level about potential opportunities because they are not involved on a daily basis with the business and don't have the same level of information available to them.

Even with all owners working in the business, owners' expectations can diverge. Some may be tolerant of risks, others may avoid risks at all costs. Some owners may want to invest money in areas such as technology, while other may want to support a certain lifestyle.

As discussed earlier, the desires of family members in different generations can also diverge. Those nearing retirement may want to take money out of the business to insure financial security while younger family members may be interested in re-investing the funds and growing the business for the future.

For these reasons, it is important that you discuss growth goals and the rationale for growth with the family. It's important to get everyone behind the reasons for and level of growth desired. Family members will need to discuss not only their objectives regarding growth, profits, and liquidity, but also the risk level they are willing to take on. All are interrelated. Realizing a desire to maximize growth often comes at the expense of other goals.

Having a facilitator help the family focus on their long-term goals may allow the family to reach decisions in a constructive manner. It may also remove you from the possible perception of promoting growth for personal reasons.

## Winning Your "Growth Team's" Commitment

Non-family managers may have expectations and desires that differ from those of family managers. Family managers have a vested interest in growing the business because they will profit in the long term. Non-family managers may not. Your management team is essentially your "growth team," the team you depend on to take your company to the next level, and you need to ensure that your non-family managers' interests line up with yours. In non-family companies, stock incentives tied to the value of the business is often used to secure the managers' commitment to growth. But it can be more difficult to align the interests of non-family managers in a family firm because ownership is almost always restricted to family members. The key is to use other kinds of incentives with non-family managers, such as bonuses linked to company performance or "phantom" stock, a form of compensation that mimics real stock without conferring actual ownership. Non-family executives need to have the opportunity for financial growth in their jobs, even if ownership is reserved for a family member.

*Your management team is essentially your "growth team," the team you depend on to take your company to the next level...*

It is also critical to share growth expectations with your managers and to include them in the planning process. They should have an opportunity to give you feedback on whether or not your goals are achievable. Family business owners often develop plans on their own without communicating those plans. This allows them to avoid commitment to a particular course of action. The surest way to get your team united behind growth is to see to it that everyone understands and buys into the plan. Going through a strategic planning process where everyone has the opportunity to express their thoughts about how to achieve growth can be very beneficial. Doing so ensures that everyone understands the goals, has a chance to take part in building the strategy and feels a personal sense of ownership in the company's future. Such participation can go a long way to getting management buy-in on your plans.

### The Role of Communication

Communication is essential to managing diverse expectations, in the family and the business, and between the two groups. Dialogues need to be carried on within the ownership group, board of directors, and management. Each group needs to share information and viewpoints with the others, ideally using the board of directors as an intermediary to communicate the owners' wishes to the management.

It may be a good idea to include certain family members who are not owners in these conversations because the decisions that are to be made could affect their lives. Spouses of owners or younger family members who someday may be owners can be allowed to air their concerns and contribute their views even though they don't have a vote on the decision. Inclusion in the discussions also educates future owners—young adults in their early 20s, about the kinds of responsibilities and decisions they will face one day and helps them develop into effective owners.

Different families have different customs, and some don't involve spouses for cultural reasons or because divorces in the family have made them sensitive about sharing information with in-laws. If your family is hesitant about including in-laws in these conversations, it is still a good idea, once the decisions are made, to communicate those decisions to them.

In a similar fashion, while you are not going to involve every level of employee in the strategic-planning process and decision making, it's important to communicate the plan to everybody once it's finalized. Employees will be on the front lines in carrying out your growth plans and will feel the stress that growth often brings. Thus, it is especially critical that they are knowledgeable about what you want to do and how you expect to do it.

## EXHIBIT 6

## *Good Venues For Conversations About Growth*

Shareholder meetings

Family meetings

Family retreats

Board meetings

Management meetings

Strategic-planning sessions

---

It's important to remember that owners set the goals for the business' growth. Family meetings are appropriate venues to develop consensus about growth and to inform family members not employed in the business as decisions are made.

The business' management team is charged with creating the plan that carries out the family's wishes for growth. At the same time it is important for the board of directors to monitor the implementation of the plan for intended results. The board assures that expectations for growth are realistic and are met.

# VIII. Are You Ready for Growth?

Here is a quick checklist of questions to ask yourself to ascertain if you are ready to pursue a growth strategy:

### Market Assessment: Is there room in the market to grow?

—Where will growth come from (new customers, new products)?

—How will competition be impacted by growth?

—Can we take advantage of growing markets?

### Management Assessment: Do we have the right people?

—Do our managers have the skills needed?

—Do they have the desire to change?

—If we need to bring in outside talent, are current managers willing to work for someone else?

—Is there expertise available on the market?

### Infrastructure Assessment: Do we have the right foundation?

—Do we have the financial, information technology, and control systems to support growth?

—Do we have replicable, scalable processes?

—Do we have the facilities required?

### Financial Assessment: Do we have the capital?

—What capital investment is required?

—What is the source of capital?

—What is its cost?

—What risk will we incur?

—What is the impact on margins?

### Ownership Assessment: Are the shareholders prepared?

—Have the owners agreed on why they want to grow the business?

—Have they arrived at a consensus about how much growth they want and how it will be achieved?

—Are the owners comfortable with the tradeoffs (i.e. paying dividends vs. re-investing profits) they must make to pursue growth?

—Are they comfortable with the risks involved?

### Family Assessment: Is our family prepared?

—Have family members been adequately informed about growth decisions?

—Have they been given an opportunity to express their concerns and offer their ideas?

—Do they understand that growth may put stress on family members, especially those working in the business?

### CEO's Self-Assessment: Am I ready?

—Am I able to embrace change?

—Am I excited about taking the company to a new level?

—Do I have the energy?

—Can I let go of control if that's what's needed?

# IX. Hitting the Wall on Growth

Why is it easy for some companies to achieve their desire for growth and difficult for others? A comparison of two successful family businesses demonstrates what it takes to achieve growth.

On the surface, these two companies have much in common. They have similar manufacturing operations and similar histories, with both nearing succession from the first to second generation. Both have grown successfully in the past and have similar growth aspirations for the future. Each has a rigorous strategic planning process through which both have developed detailed plans outlining the steps they will take to accomplish growth. These steps are both realistic and attainable. So, why is one business exceeding its growth expectations while the other is having difficulty matching the performance it achieved the previous year?

Let's look at what is different about these companies. First, GrowthCo is larger and older than NoGrowthCo. Second, GrowthCo is the market leader in a business with strong brand recognition and high margins. NoGrowthCo is a local player in a market dominated by one major national player where competition focuses on price and margins are thin. Third, GrowthCo has recently brought in new senior management with experience outside its industry. NoGrowthCo has brought in a couple of new managers, but most members of the team have worked their entire careers at NoGrowthCo and the new hires are all industry veterans.

Why do these differences translate into a difference in the ability to grow?

## Age, Size and Growth

Most businesses grow through a natural evolution. When the business is started, the entrepreneur/founder does whatever it takes to get the business off the ground. Management is very hands-on, involved in every aspect of daily operations. People don't worry about whether or not the process to get the product out the door is the most efficient—they are just concerned with survival. In the entrepreneurial stage, determination and hard work make the business successful.

As the business grows, systems and processes must be established so that tasks can be accomplished consistently. This consistency is important to ensure the quality of products and services. Increased efficiency allows management to spend less time thinking about daily operations and more time about the future. Managers are able to delegate responsibility to employees who work for them because they can be assured that the business will operate effectively, even if they are not involved in every aspect of daily operations. Companies that reach this phase have transitioned to a professional organization.

GrowthCo, being larger and older, has already successfully transformed itself into a professional organization. NoGrowthCo is still in the entrepreneurial phase. So why hasn't NoGrowthCo made the transition?

The number one reason that companies do not make this transition is that they do not recognize the need for change. They understand that the way they have done business in the past has allowed them to grow and be successful, so they don't see a need to do anything different. Even if they are aware of the need, human beings generally resist change. Unless they are dealing with a crisis, many managers will maintain the status quo. Some characteristics of family businesses make this problem even more prevalent. As noted earlier, family members in the business often have never worked anywhere else, so they can't imagine another way of doing things. Or, the founding generation may resist the next generation's suggestions that things should be different. They see the desire for change as a challenge to their authority, legacy and financial security.

## Level of Competition

Beyond size and age, our two companies operate in different markets. GrowthCo is in a much less competitive market, which gives it several advantages over NoGrowthCo. GrowthCo has the luxury to think about the long term, while NoGrowthCo cannot afford to make mistakes; every mistake it makes provides an opening for the competition to attack its market.

GrowthCo actually made several mistakes as it was growing through the transition from an entrepreneurial company to a professional organization. It made a couple of bad acquisitions and hired some senior managers that weren't a good fit. It was able to recover from these mistakes, however, without serious harm to the business. Thanks to healthy margins, it was able to overcome the financial cost of these errors.

Does this suggest that in order to grow successfully, you need to be in a high-margin business with little competition? Not at all. In fact, companies in competitive markets need to be even more proactive about making the changes needed to achieve growth. If the changes aren't made ahead of growth, problems caused by growth pains can invite opportunities for competitive attack. Case in point: NoGrowthCo did not recognize that it needed to streamline operating and customer-service processes in order to serve the additional customers required to achieve its growth goals. As a result, product quality and customer service suffered and its customer retention rate dropped.

## Bringing in New Players

One last distinction between GrowthCo and NoGrowthCo is the difference in their management teams. You will recall that GrowthCo's senior managers had experience outside the company's industry, while NoGrowthCo hired industry veterans or promoted from within the ranks of key managers with limited or no outside experience. As a result,

GrowthCo's senior management recognized the need to change systems and processes to achieve its growth objectives. NoGrowthCo's team was slow to see the need for change. No one on the team had ever managed the kind of change required.

Here are five tips to keep from falling into the NoGrowthCo trap:

### 1. Recognize the need for change.

Just because the way you do business has been successful in the past doesn't mean it will take you where you want to go. Take a close look at the areas which are most challenging. Those are the areas you need to consider changing. Make sure you dig into the root cause of the problems. Problems may surface in customer service, but, the true cause of the problem may be in operations, which is delivering a poor-quality product.

> *Just because the way you do business has been successful in the past doesn't mean it will take you where you want to go.*

### 2. Invest in people.

Do a thorough assessment of your management team. Do your senior people have the skills, experience and desire to manage the transition from an entrepreneurial company to a professional organization? You need people who:

—embrace, rather than resist, change;

—consider different ways of doing things;

—have the energy and creativity to investigate different ways of doing things and test them to see if they will work; and

—are capable of delegating responsibility to their subordinates and managing their performance to ensure that they deliver results.

### 3. Put an infrastructure in place that will allow you to grow.

People are not the only change you may need to make. You need to look closely at how you're doing things. Can your key operating processes be replicated consistently day in and day out, or do they require constant management intervention? Becoming a professional organization requires putting systems and procedures in place that produce the same results every time.

### 4. Get managers out of daily operations.

To grow, management must focus its energy on creating a plan to achieve its growth goals. If management spends all or most of its time focusing on daily operations, no one is focusing on growth. A rule of thumb is that senior management should spend 80 percent of its time thinking about strategic, long-term issues and 20 percent on daily operations. The higher you rise in the organization, the more time and effort should be spent on the long term.

Even when the systems and processes are put in place that allow managers to think about the long term, some stay rooted in day-to-day decision making. They either don't have the desire or they lack the skills to think about the long term or thinking about day-to-day issues is so ingrained that they have a tough time changing their behavior. Sometimes they are not comfortable delegating to their subordinates because these managers know they will ultimately be responsible for results.

The best way to get senior managers out of this trap is to engage them in long-term planning and assign them long-term projects. If you set and hold expectations that these long-term projects will be delivered, senior managers will not have the time to focus on daily operations. In some cases, if you find that senior managers are not able to make the leap to this new management style, they may have to be replaced, or another manager may need to be hired above them.

### 5. Get an outside perspective.

It is always useful to engage the expertise of individuals who have seen operations outside your own. You don't need to reinvent the wheel in creating replicable systems and processes. There are thousands of companies, and employees of those companies, that have done it before. Get them to help you. Add outside members to your advisory board or board of directors who have experience in managing the kind of growth you hope to achieve. Many industry associations support interaction among their members. Organize benchmarking visits to businesses in your industry that are outside your market territory to see how they operate. Make sure your children get experience outside your company or industry before they join the family firm. Hire a consultant to help you identify and implement needed changes.

Making the transition from an entrepreneurial business to a professional organization is one of the toughest challenges that younger businesses face. Many do not survive the transition. But, if you recognize the need for change, enlist the help of individuals who support this change and are not afraid of the future (mistakes and all), you will be able to achieve continuous growth.

> *Making the transition from an entrepreneurial business to a professional organization is one of the toughest challenges that younger businesses face.*

# X. The Dynamics Will Change

*The challenges of growth change with each new generation.*

The challenges of growth change with each new generation. The business environment will be different. The skill sets, personalities and management styles of the family members working in the business will be different. What family members need and want from the business will shift over time and so will family members' relationship to the enterprise.

Business founders may have wonderful characteristics that enable them to launch a business, but, often they do not have the skills necessary to grow it. A son, daughter, sibling or cousin team or a non-family executive may have to take on that challenge.

As a business becomes older, it tends to become more professionalized and, as a result, better able to grow. The systems are in place that reduces the need for doing things "manually," and managers' time becomes available for more strategic thinking.

In later generations, growth to provide liquidity will become more of an issue. In its early years, a family firm may have only one shareholder—the founder. As the business transitions, there may be more family member owners and only some of whom may be employed in the business. Family members will be more diverse in beliefs and occupations, and will, quite likely, be more geographically scattered. Pressures for higher dividends or the desire to cash out will increase, competing for the money the company needs for growth. Some family members may be less committed to continuing as owners.

Older, larger family businesses usually reflect a much different organizational structure. There may now be a formal board of directors, comprised of independent, outside members and family members. The board may have a strategic planning committee to help the business prepare for growth. An annual shareholders meeting may be used to communicate growth plans and other vital information.

In later generations, the family may establish its own governance structure, creating a family council to help the family manage its relationship to the business. The family may establish committees to address such issues as communication, family employment in the business, and philanthropy. By this time, the family may have instituted a more structured program for educating younger family members for ownership.

A recent study by Matthew C. Sonfield and Robert N. Lussier compares first, second-, and third-generation family businesses and further illustrates the differences between early- and later-stage companies.[11] The researchers' findings suggest that subsequent-generation family firms are more likely than first-generation family businesses to:

- include non-family members in top management;

- have women family members working in the business;

- use a team-management approach to management;

- experience conflict and disagreement among family members;

- develop succession plans;

- use outside consultants, advisors and professional services;

- focus more on strategic management activities;

- use sophisticated methods of financial management, and;

- have considered going public.

All of these characteristics impact growth one way or another. The inclusion of women and non-family managers can increase the talent pool to grow the business. Reliance on outside consultants and more sophisticated management tools can enhance business growth, while conflict and disagreement in the family can inhibit it. It's helpful for business leaders to look at the road ahead, initiating positive change and taking steps to mitigate inevitable problems.

Just as change comes to the world outside, so does change come to the family and its business. To resist it courts disaster. To embrace it and capitalize on it is often the path to survival.

EXHIBIT 7

# *How Family Firms Change Across Generations*

## First Generation

Business has one or few owners.

Owner's skills lend themselves to starting a business.

Business is likely to be run by an authoritarian leader.

Owner/leader focuses on day-to-day operations.

All family members work in the business.

There is no outside board of directors.

## Later Generations

Business has many shareholders.

Owners' skills enable them to grow the company.

The business is run by a team.

Leaders focus on strategic management activities.

Relatively few family members work in the business.

The business has a board with independent outsiders.

The business may have formed a family council.

# XI. Summary

*Choosing to grow, should not be purely for the sake of growth but for solid reasons, such as staying competitive or enabling your business to provide liquidity to family shareholders.*

Some family business owners pursue growth with energy and passion. They are convinced that growth is good for the business, the owning family, and the community. In addition, these owners simply find it fun to make their businesses grow.

Other owners are more comfortable keeping their family businesses small. The rush that some business leaders get from rapid expansion is not for them. They prefer to maintain a manageable, profitable size that meets the owners' needs without too much risk. They like knowing all their employees by their first names, and fear something important would be lost if their companies were larger.

**To grow or not to grow?** Whatever you decide can be appropriate, as long as you thoroughly understand the reasons and implications for your choice. Choosing to grow, should not be purely for the sake of growth but for solid reasons, such as staying competitive or enabling your business to provide liquidity to family shareholders. Deciding to stay small, should not be done out of complacency or the feeling that you can be successful in the future by doing what made you successful in the past. Again, it's wise to develop a rationale for staying small. Perhaps being a modest-sized family firm distinguishes you from your competitors or enables you to provide a level of service that you could not offer if you were larger.

Family business owners can also consider different definitions of growth. Usually we think of growth in terms of revenues or profits, but there are other ways to look at it. Growth can be measured by improvements in products or services, efficiencies in processes or increases in the number of employees. A company can stay small in terms of revenues but still grow by getting better at what it does.

Once family business owners decide they want to grow, they must be able to answer several

*Deciding to stay small, should not be done out of complacency or the feeling that you can be successful in the future by doing what made you successful in the past.*

53

other critical questions: How much growth is right for us? Is our business capable of the growth we want? If not, can we make it capable and, if so, how?

Answering such questions requires considerable analyses of the business as well as many healthy conversations within and between groups of stakeholders: management, shareholders, other family members and the board of directors. There will be some disagreement when people's needs or wants conflict with those of others or with growth itself—as the desire of some shareholders for higher dividends might conflict with the desire of others to invest profits in a new facility. In time, most business-owning families reach a consensus about growth and how to achieve it.

Considerable thought will need to be given to where your company's growth will come from. It makes sense to begin with existing customer segments, focusing first on improving customer retention, increasing market share, and capitalizing on market growth. Selling more of your current products or services to existing customer segments is usually the easiest and cheapest way to grow. But for some businesses, it may be necessary to take bolder steps, identifying new market segments for existing products, offering new product extensions for existing customers, or offering new products to new customers.

Business owners will also have to commit resources needed to support growth, putting together a management team that can take the company to the next level. They also need to put the necessary infrastructure in place in terms of facilities and technology as well as processes and systems. Finally they need to make sure that their financing is adequate.

Growth goals need to be realistic and achievable. And once the growth effort has been launched, follow-up is essential to see if you are meeting your goals. It's a good idea to set plan to paper so that you have something to measure against. If the plan is not working, make the necessary adjustments or do something else.

All the stakeholders need to understand that decisions about growth require tradeoffs. When you pursue growth, for example, you may have to borrow money, something many business-owning families don't like to do. When you elect to remain smaller, you may be giving up opportunities for greater wealth or the ability to employ more people.

If you elect to grow, however, remember that it's healthy growth you're after—growth that is sustainable and profitable. Achieving growth is challenging and it can be risky, but it can also be richly rewarding and exciting. Staying small, which also carries risks, can offer pleasures and rewards of its own. Thoughtfully deciding what is right for you is the key. Isn't it wonderful to have the choice?

# Notes

1. Cooper, Porus P. "Wawa Isn't All in the Family," *The Philadelphia Inquirer*, Nov. 7, 2004, pp. E1, E8.

2. Phillips, Angus. "Fletcher Family's Potomac Journey Nears an End," *The Washington Post*, Nov. 4, 2004, p. A1.

3. Treacy, Michael. *Double-Digit Growth: How Great Companies Achieve It—No Matter What*. New York: Penguin Group, 2003, p. 3.

4. "Keeping the Family Business Small." *Family Business Advisor®*, Volume 8, Issue 9 (September 2004), p. 7.

5. Hoover, Edwin A. "Biggest Isn't Always Best," *Family Business*, Volume 14, Number 2 (Spring 2003), pp. 30-33.

6. Nelton, Sharon. "Coming to Grips with Growth." *Nation's Business*, Volume 86, No. 2 (February 1998), pp. 26-32.

7. Brubaker, Harold. "Acquisitions More Than Double Size of Alderfer." *The Philadelphia Inquirer*, Aug. 23, 2004, pp. E1, E12.

8. "The Best & Worst Managers of the Year." *Business Week*, Jan. 10, 2005, pp. 55-86.

9. Charan, Ram. *Profitable Growth Is Everyone's Business: 10 Tools You Can Use Monday Morning*. New York: Crown Business, 2004, p. 28.

10. Clifford, Donald K., Jr., and Richard E. Cavanagh. *The Winning Performance: How America's High-growth Midsize Companies Succeed*. Toronto: Bantam Books, 1988, p. 13.

11. Sonfield, Matthew C., and Robert N. Lussier. "First-, Second-, and Third-Generation Family Firms: A Comparison." *Family Business Review*, Volume 17, Number 3 (September 2004), pp.189-202.

# Suggested Additional Readings

Aronoff, Craig E. and John L. Ward. *Family Business Governance: Maximizing Family and Business Potential*, Marietta, GA: Family Enterprise Publishers®, 1996.

Aronoff, Craig E. and John L. Ward. *Family Business Ownership: How to be an Effective Shareholder*, Marietta, GA: Family Enterprise Publishers®, 2002.

Aronoff, Craig E. and John L. Ward. *Family Meetings: How to Build a Stronger Family and a Stronger Business*, 2nd edition. Marietta, GA: Family Enterprise Publishers®, 2002.

Aronoff, Craig E. and John L. Ward. *Make Change Your Family Business Tradition*, Marietta, GA: Family Enterprise Publishers®, 2001.

Carlock, Randel S., and John L. Ward. *Strategic Planning for the Family Business: Parallel Planning To Unify the Family and Business*, New York: Palgrave, 2001.

Charan, Ram. *Profitable Growth Is Everyone's Business: 10 Tools You Can Use Monday Morning*, New York: Crown Business, 2004.

Clifford, Donald K., Jr., and Richard E. Cavanagh. *The Winning Performance: How America's High-growth Midsize Companies Succeed*, Toronto: Bantam Books, 1988.

Eckrich, Christopher J. and Stephen L. McClure. *Working for a Family Business: A Non-Family Employee's Guide to Success*, Marietta, GA: Family Enterprise Publishers®, 2004.

Poza, Ernesto J. *Smart Growth: Critical Choices for Business Continuity and Prosperity*, San Francisco: Jossey-Bass, 1989.

Treacy, Michael. *Double-Digit Growth: How Great Companies Achieve It—No Matter What*, New York: Penguin Group, 2003.

# The Author

## Jennifer M. Pendergast, Ph.D.

Dr. Pendergast is the Family Development Manager for RFA Management Company, a large family office and was a senior associate of The Family Business Consulting Group, Inc.®.

Her research on corporate governance and top management leadership issues has been published in a number of academic journals, including *European Management Journal* and *Strategic Management Journal*. She completed research on the impact of board structure and composition on corporate performance for her doctoral dissertation.

Jennifer received her Ph.D. in Management from Wharton Business School and holds a B.S. in Finance from University of Virginia's McIntire School of Commerce.

Jennifer serves on the board of the Fulton County Juvenile Justice Fund and is past president of Community Consulting Teams. She is married, the mother of twins and resides in Atlanta.

# Index